On Union
with God

Faith, Hope and Charity. Drawing by John Flaxman. Based on an engraving by Thomas Piroli (1793) to illustrate the beginning of *Paradise* from Dante's *The Divine Comedy*.

Ways of Mysticism

On Union
with God

ALBERT THE GREAT

CONTINUUM

About the illustrations
The two illustrations which open each chapter are: *The Holy Ghost as a Dove*. An engraving by Eric Gill by kind permission of the Board of Trustees of the Victoria & Albert Museum; and a drawing based on a fifth-century bronze cross with monogram chi-rho and the symbols 'alpha' and 'omega'.

The Publishers would like to thank the following for permission to reproduce illustrations: Board of Trustees of the Victoria & Albert Museum: pp. 27, 70, 77, 89; e.t. archive: pp.29,33,50,55: National Gallery of Scotland: p. 66.

Continuum Publishing Inc.
Wellington House, 125 Strand, London WC2R 0BB
320 Lexington Avenue, New York, NY 10017-6550, USA

This edition first published in 1911 by Burns Oates & Washbourne

First published 2000 in the Ways of Mysticism Series

ISBN 0826449980

A · Delian · Bower · Book
Edited, designed and produced by
Delian Bower Publishing
Exeter England

Designed by Vic Giolitto
Picture research by Anne-Marie Ehrlich

Printed in China

Contents

Foreword

D*e adhaerendo Deo* or *On Union with God* written by Albert the Great (Albertus Magnus) during the twelfth century best expresses his own personal mysticism.

If God is a Spirit, to be worshipped in spirit, the mind must be cleared of images, the doors of the senses must be shut. The mind freed from distractions is in some sense transformed into God.

Commonly called the Universal Doctor and placed by Dante among the lovers of wisdom, he was beatified in 1622 and canonised in 1931, when he was named by Pope Pius XI both as a Doctor of the Church and the patron of students of natural sciences. His Feastday is on 15th November.

The present translation by a Benedictine of Princethorpe Priory was first published in 1911. Some small revisions have been made to the text but the spirit of the original has been retained. The biblical references unless otherwise stated are from the Revised Standard Version of the Bible. Old Testament references, Copyright © HarperCollins 1952. New Testament References, Copyright © HarperCollins 1971.

The notes included at the end of each chapter which were included in the 1911 edition are by Revd. P J Berthier OP (from the French edition: *De l'Union avec Dieu*).

The Holy Trinity. Woodcut by Albrecht Dürer (1471-1528)

Preface

Surely the most deeply-rooted need of the human soul, its purest aspiration, is for the closest possible union with God. As you turn over the pages of this little work, written by Blessed Albert the Great[1] towards the end of his life, when that great soul had ripened and matured, you feel that here indeed is the ideal of your hopes.

Simply and clearly the great principles are laid down, the way is made plain which leads to the highest spiritual life. It seems as though, while you read, the mists of earth vanish and the snowy summits appear of the mountains of God. We breathe only the pure atmosphere of prayer, peace, and love, and the one great fact of the universe, the Divine Presence, is felt and realized without effort.

But is such a life possible amid the whirl of the twenty-first century? To faith and love all things are possible, and our author shows us the loving Father, ever ready to give as much and more than we can ask. The spirit of such a work is ever true; the application may vary with circumstances, but the guidance of the Holy Spirit will never be wanting to those souls who crave for closer union with their Divine Master.

This little treatise has been very aptly called the 'Metaphysics of the Imitation,' and it is in the hope that it may be of use to souls that it has been translated into English.

Blessed Albert the Great is too well known for it to be necessary for us to give more than the briefest outline of his life.

Gazing for an instant at the point of light which is God.
Drawing by John Flaxman to illustrate Canto Twenty-Nine of *Paradise* from
Dante's *The Divine Comedy*.

The eldest son of the Count of Bollstädt, he was born at Lauingen in Swabia in 1205 or 1206, though some historians give it as 1193. As a youth he was sent to the University of Padua, where he had special facilities for the study of the liberal arts.

Drawn by the persuasive teaching of Blessed Jordan of Saxony, he joined the Order of St. Dominic in 1223, and after completing his studies, received the Doctor's degree at the University of Paris.

His brilliant genius quickly brought him into the most prominent positions. Far-famed for his learning, he attracted scholars from parts of Europe to Paris, Cologne, Ratisbon, etc., where he successively taught. It was during his years of teaching at Paris and Cologne that he counted among his disciples St. Thomas Aquinas, the greatness of whose future he foretold, and whose lifelong friendship with him then began.

In 1254 Albert was elected Provincial of his Order in Germany. In 1260 he was appointed Bishop of Ratisbon, but resigned his see in 1262. He then continued unweriedly until a few years before his death, when his great powers, especially his memory, failed him, but the fervour of his soul remained ever the same. In 1280, at Cologne, he sank, at last worn out by his manifold labours.

'Whether we consider him as a theologian or as a philosopher, Albert was undoubtedly one of the most extraordinary men of his age; I might say, one of the most wonderful men of genius who appeared in past times' (Jourdain).

Very grateful thanks are due to Revd. P. J. Berthier, O.P., for his kind permission to append to this edition a translation of his excellent notes (from the French edition, entitled *De l'Union avec Dieu*).

NOTES

[1] Following the general tradition, we attribute this work to Albert the Great, but not all critics are agreed as to its authenticity.

CHAPTER 1

Of the Highest Perfection which Man can reach in this Life

have felt moved to write a few last thoughts describing, as far as one may in this waiting-time of our exile and pilgrimage, the entire separation of the soul from all earthly things and its close, unfettered union with God.

I have been the more urged to this, because Christian perfection has no other end but love, which unites us to God.[1]

This union of love is essential for salvation, since it consists in the practice of the precepts and in conformity to the Divine will. Hence it separates us from whatever would war against the essence and habit of charity, such as mortal sin.[2]

But religious, the more easily to attain to God, their last end, have gone beyond this, and have bound themselves by vow to evangelical perfection, to that which is voluntary and of counsel.[3] With the help of these vows they cut off all that might impede the fervour of their love or hinder them in their flight to God. They have, therefore, by the vow of their religious profession, renounced all things, whether pertaining to soul or body.[4] God is Spirit, and 'those that worship Him must worship Him in spirit and in truth,'[5] that is, with a knowledge and love, an intelligence and will purified from every phantom of earth.

Hence it is written: 'But when you pray, go into your room'—*i.e.*, into the inmost abode of your heart—and, 'shut the door' of your senses, with a pure heart, a free conscience and an unfeigned faith, 'and pray to your Father in secret'.[6]

Then only will a man attain to this ideal, when he has stripped himself of all else; when, wholly recollected within himself, he has hidden from and forgotten the whole world, that he may abide in silence in the presence of Jesus Christ. There, in solitude of soul, with loving confidence he makes known his desires to God. With all the intensity of his love he pours forth his heart before Him, in sincerity and truth, until he loses himself in God. Then is his heart enlarged, inflamed, and melted in him, yea, even in its inmost depths.

NOTES

[1] Albert the Great is speaking here in a special manner of religious perfection, although what he says is also true of Christian perfection in general.

[2] He speaks here of the obligation laid upon all Christians.

[3] Religious bind themselves to observe as a duty that which was only of counsel. To them, therefore, the practice of the counsels of perfection(namely poverty, chastity, and obedience) becomes an obligation.

[4] The vows of religion have as their immediate object the removal of obstacles to perfection, but they do not in themselves constitute perfection. Perfection consists in charity. Albert the Great speaks of only one vow, because in his day the formulas of religious profession mentioned only the vow of obedience, which includes the other two vows.

[5] John 4, 24.

[6] Matt 6, 6.

Symbol of Faith, Hope and Love.

CHAPTER 2

How You May Despise All Things and Cling to Christ Alone

Whoever you are who longs to enter upon this happy state or seeks to direct your steps, it is well for you to act.

First, close, as it were, your eyes, and bar the doors of your senses. Suffer not anything to entangle your soul, nor permit any care or trouble to penetrate within it.

Shake off all earthly things, counting them useless, noxious, and hurtful to you.[1]

When you have done this, enter wholly within yourself, and fix your gaze upon the wounded Jesus, and upon Him alone. Strive with all your powers, unwearyingly, to reach God through Himself, that is, through God made Man, that you may attain to the knowledge of His Divinity through the wounds of His Sacred Humanity.

In all simplicity and confidence abandon yourself and

Vision of Jesus crucified. Drawing by John Flaxman to illustrate Canto Fourteen of *Paradise* from Dante's *The Divine Comedy.*

whatever concerns you without reserve to God's unfailing Providence, according to the teaching of St. Peter: 'Cast all your anxieties on Him,'[2] Who can do all things. And again it is written: 'Have no anxiety about anything;'[3] 'Cast your burden on the Lord and He will sustain you';[4] 'It is good for me to be near God';[5] 'I keep the Lord always before me';[6] 'I found Him whom my soul loves'.[7] This is the hidden and heavenly treasure, the precious pearl, which is to be preferred before all. This it is that we must seek with humble confidence and untiring effort, yet in silence and peace.

It must be sought with a brave heart, even though its price be the loss of bodily comfort, of esteem, and of honour.

Lacking this, what does it profit a religious if he 'gains the whole world, and forfeits his life?'[8] Of what value are the religious state, the holiness of our profession, the shaven head, the outward signs of a life of abnegation, if we lack the spirit of humility and truth, in which Christ dwells by faith and love? St. Luke says: 'The kingdom of God,' that is, Christ, 'is in the midst of you.'[9]

Notes

[1] When Albert the Great and the other mystics warn us against solicitude with regard to creatures, they refer to that solicitude which is felt for creatures in themselves; they do not mean that we ought not to occupy ourselves with them in any way for God's sake. The great doctor explains his meaning in clear terms later on in this work.

[2] 1 Pet. 5. 7.   [3] Phil. 4. 6.

[4] Ps. 55. 22.   [5] Ps. 73. 28.   [6] Ps. 16. 8.   [7] Song of Sol. 3. 4.

[8] Matt, 16. 26.

[9] Luke 17. 21.

CHAPTER 3

Perfection in
this Life

In proportion as the mind is absorbed in the thought and care of the things of this world do we lose the fervour of our devotion, and drift away from the things of Heaven.

The greater, on the other hand, our diligence in withdrawing our powers from the memory, love and thought of that which is inferior in order to fix them upon that which is above, the more perfect will be our prayer, the purer our contemplation. The soul cannot give itself perfectly at the same time to two objects as contrary one to another as light to darkness;[1] for he who lives united to God dwells in the light, he who clings to this world lives in darkness.

The highest perfection, therefore, of man in this life lies in this: that he is so united to God that his soul with all its powers and faculties becomes immersed in Him and is one spirit with Him.[2] Then it remembers nothing but God, nor does it relish or understand anything but Him. Then all its affections, united in the delights of love, repose sweetly in the enjoyment of their Creator.

The image of God which is imprinted upon the soul is found in the three powers of the reason, memory, and will. But since these do not perfectly bear the Divine likeness, they have not the same resemblance to God as in the first days of man's creation.[3]

God is the 'form' of the soul upon which He must impress His own image, as the seal on the wax or the stamp on the object it marks.[4]

This can only be fully accomplished when the reason is wholly illuminated according to its capacity, by the knowledge of God, the Sovereign Truth; the will entirely devoted to the love of the Supreme Good; the memory absorbed in the contemplation and enjoyment of eternal happiness, and in the sweet repose of so great a state.

As the perfect possession of this state constitutes the glory of the Blessed in Heaven, it is clear that in its commencement consists the perfection of this life.

NOTES

[1] Albert the Great supposes here that we give ourselves equally to God and to creatures, which would be wrong, and not that creatures are subordinated to God, which would be a virtue.

[2] This must be understood to mean that God is the principal and supreme end of all created activities.

[3] The perfect image of God in man does not consist merely in the possession of those faculties by which we resemble Him, but rather in performing by faith and love, as far as is in our power, acts like those which He performs, in knowing Him as He knows Himself, in loving Him as He loves Himself.

[4] In scholastic theology the term 'form' is used of that which gives to anything its accidental or substantial being. God is the 'accidental form' of the soul, because in giving it its activity He bestows upon it something of His own activity, by means of sanctifying grace. Yet more truly may it be said that God is also the 'form' of the soul in the sense that it is destined by the ordinary workings of Providence to participate by sanctifying grace in the Being of God, enjoying thus a participation real, though created, in the Divine nature.

CHAPTER 4

That our Concern must be with the Understanding and not with the Senses

Blessed is he who by continually cleansing his soul from the images and distractions of earth draws its powers inward, and thereby lifts them up to God.

At length he in a manner forgets all images, and by a simple and direct act of pure intellect and will contemplates God, Who is absolutely simple.

Cast from you, therefore, all distractions, images, and forms, and whatsoever is not God,[1] that all your intercourse with Him may proceed from an understanding, affection, and will, alike purified. This is, in truth, the end of all your labours, that you may draw closer to God and repose in Him within your soul, solely by your understanding and by a fervent love, free from entanglement or earthly image.

Not by his bodily organs or outward senses does a man attain to this, but by the intelligence and will, which constitute him man.[2] So long as he lingers, trifling with the objects of the imagination and senses, he has not yet passed beyond the limits and instincts of his animal nature, which he possesses in common with the animals. They know and feel through images and by their senses, nor can it be otherwise, for they have no higher powers. Not so is it with man, who, by his intelligence, affections, and will, is created in the image and likeness of God. Hence it is by these powers that he ought, without intermediary, purely and directly to commune with God, be united to Him, and cling to Him.[3]

The Devil does his very utmost to hinder us from this exercise, for he sees in it a beginning and a foretaste of eternal life, and he is envious of man. Therefore he strives, now by one temptation or passion, now by another, to turn away our thoughts from God.

At one time he assails us by arousing in us unnecessary anxiety, foolish cares or troubles, or by drawing us to

The Shepherd. Engraving by Samuel Palmer (1805-81). Visionary and mystical landscape painter.

irregular conversations and vain curiosity. At another he ensnares us by subtle books, by the words of others, by rumours and novelties. Then, again, he has recourse to trials, contradictions, etc.

Although these things may sometimes seem but very trifling faults, if faults at all, yet do they greatly hinder our progress in this holy exercise. Therefore, whether great or small, they must be resisted and driven from us as evil and harmful, though they may seem useful and even necessary. It is of great importance that what we have heard, or seen, or done, or said, should not leave their traces or fill our imagination.

Neither before nor after, nor at the time, should we foster these memories or allow their images to be formed. For when the mind is free from these thoughts, we are not hindered in our prayer, in meditation, or the reading of the psalms, or in any other of our spiritual exercises, nor do these distractions return to trouble us.

Then you should readily and trustfully commit yourself and all that concerns you to the unfailing and most sure Providence of God, in silence and peace. He Himself will fight for you, and will grant you a liberty and consolation better, nobler, and sweeter than would be possible if you gave yourself up day and night to your fancies, to vain and wandering thoughts, which hold captive the mind, as they toss it hither and thither, wearying soul and body, and wasting uselessly alike your time and strength.[4]

Accept all things, whatsoever their cause, silently and with a tranquil mind, as coming to you from the fatherly hand of Divine Providence.

Free yourself, therefore, from all the impressions of earthly things, in so far as your state and profession require, so that with a purified mind and sincere affection you may cling to Him to Whom you have so often and so entirely vowed yourself.

Let nothing remain which could come between your soul and God, that so you may be able to pass surely and directly from the wounds of the Sacred Humanity to the brightness of the Divinity.

NOTES

[1] We must avoid these things in so far as they separate us from God, but they may also serve to draw us nearer to Him if we regard them in God and for God.

[2] It is by the intelligence and will that man actually attains to this, but the use of the sensitive faculties is presupposed.

[3] The sensitive faculties, if used as a means, often help us to draw near to God, but when used as an end, their activity becomes an obstacle.

[4] This teaching is the Christian rendering of the axiom formulated by the Philosopher: '*Homo sedendo fit sapiens*'—'It is in quiet that man gains wisdom.'

Christ enthroned. Romanesque relief of the thirteenth century.

CHAPTER 5

Of Purity of Heart, which is to be sought above All Else

Do you want to journey by the shortest road, the straight and safe way to eternal bliss, unto your true country, to grace and glory? Strive with all your might to obtain habitual cleanness of heart, purity of mind, quiet of the senses. Gather up your affections, and with your whole heart cling to God.

Withdraw as much as you can from your acquaintances and from all men, and abstain from such affairs as would hinder your purpose.

Seek out with jealous care the place, time, and means most suited to quiet and contemplation, and lovingly embrace silence and solitude.

Beware the dangers of which the times are full; avoid the agitation of a world never at rest, never still.[1]

Let your chief study be to gain purity, freedom, and peace of heart. Close the doors of your senses and dwell within, shutting your heart as diligently as you can against the shapes and images of earthly things.

Of all the practices of the spiritual life purity of heart stands highest, and rightly, for it is the end and reward of all our labours, and is found only with those who live truly according to the spirit and as good religious.

Wherefore you should employ all your diligence and skill in order to free your heart, senses, and affections from whatever could trammel their liberty, or could restrain or ensnare your soul. Strive earnestly to gather in the wandering affections of your heart and fix them on the love of the sole and pure Truth, the Sovereign Good; then keep them, as it were, enchained within you.

Fix your gaze unwaveringly upon God and Divine things; spurn the follies of earth and seek to be wholly transformed in Jesus Christ, yea, even to the heart's core.

When you have begun to cleanse and purify your soul of earthly images, and to unify and tranquillize your heart and mind in God with loving confidence, to the end that

Mosaic of the four evangelists, Matthew, Mark, Luke and John
with their symbols. Sixth century.

you may taste and enjoy in all your powers the torrents of His good pleasure, and may fix your will and intelligence in Him, then you will no longer need to study and read the Holy Scriptures to learn the love of God and of your neighbour, for the Holy Spirit Himself will teach you.[2]

Spare no pains, no labour, to purify your heart and to establish it in unbroken peace.

Abide in God in the secret place of your soul as tranquilly as though there had already risen upon you the dawn of Eternity, the unending Day of God.

Strong in the love of Jesus, go forth from yourself, with a heart pure, a conscience at peace, a faith unfeigned; and in every trial, every event, commit yourself unreservedly to God, having nothing so much at heart as perfect obedience to His will and good pleasure.

If you get this far, you should often enter within your soul and abide there, disengaging yourself as much as you can from all things.

Keep the eye of your soul ever in purity and peace; suffer not the form and images of this world to defile your mind; preserve your will from every earthly care, and let every fibre of your heart be rooted in the love of the Sovereign Good. Then your whole soul, with all its powers, be recollected in God and form but one spirit with Him.

It is in this that the highest perfection possible to man here below consists.

This union of the spirit and of love, by which a man conforms himself in everything to the supreme and eternal will, enables us to become by grace what God is by His nature.[3]

Let us not forget this truth: the moment a man, by the help of God, succeeds in overcoming his own will, that is, in freeing himself from every inordinate affection and care, to cast himself and all his miseries unreservedly into the bosom of God, that moment he becomes so pleasing to God that he receives the gift of grace. Grace brings love, and love drives out all fear and hesitation, and fills the soul with confidence and hope. What is more blessed than to call all our care on Him Who cannot fail? As long as you lean upon yourself you will totter. Throw yourself without fear into the arms of God. He will embrace you, He will heal and save you.[4]

If you think often of these truths they would bring to you more happiness than all the riches, delights, honours, of this false world, and would make you more blessed than all the wisdom and knowledge of this corruptible life, even though you should surpass all the wise men who have gone before you.

NOTES

[1] This is especially true for religious.

[2] By this is meant that the Holy Scriptures, though always presupposed as the foundation of our belief, of themselves give only an objective knowledge of God, while that which the Holy Ghost gives is experimental.

[3] God knows and loves Himself in Himself by His own nature, while we know and love Him in Himself by grace.

[4] A very striking feature in the doctrine of this book is that it requires first the perfection of the soul and the faculties, whence proceeds that of our actions. Some modern authors, confining themselves to casuistry, speak almost exclusively of the perfection of actions, a method less logical and less thorough.

CHAPTER 6

That a Man Truly Devout must seek God in Purity of Mind and Heart

As you go forward in this work of ridding yourself of every earthly thought and entanglement you will notice your soul regain her strength and the mastery of her inward senses, and you will begin to taste the sweetness of heavenly things.

Learn, therefore, to keep yourself free from the images of outward and material objects, for God loves with a special love the soul that is consequently purified. His 'delights' are 'delighting in the sons of men,'[1] that is, with those who, set free from earthly affairs and distractions, and at peace from their passions, offer Him simple and pure hearts intent on Him alone.

If the memory, imagination, and thoughts still dwell below, it follows of necessity that fresh events, memories of the past, and other things will ensnare and drag you down. But the Holy Spirit is not in such empty thoughts.

The true friend of Jesus Christ must be so united by his intelligence and will to the Divine will and goodness that his imagination and passions have no hold over him, and that he troubles not whether men give him love or ridicule, nor heeds what may be done to him. Know well that a truly good will does all and is of more value than all.

If the will is good, wholly conformed and united to God, and guided by reason, it matters little that the flesh, the senses, the exterior man are inclined to evil and sluggish in good, or even that a man find himself interiorly lacking in devotion.[2] It suffices that he remains with his whole soul inwardly united to God by faith and a good will.

This he will accomplish if, knowing his own imperfection and utter nothingness, he understands that all his happiness is in his Creator. Then does he forsake himself, his own strength and powers, and every creature, and hides himself in complete abandonment in the bosom of God.

To God are all his actions simply and purely directed. He seeks nothing outside of God, but knows that of a truth he has found in Him all the good and all the happiness of perfection. Then will he be in some measure transformed in God. He will no longer be able to think, love, understand, remember anything except God and the things of God. He will no longer see himself or creatures except in God; no love will possess him but the love of God, nor will he remember creatures or even his own being, except in God.

Such a knowledge of the truth renders the soul humble, makes her a hard judge towards herself, but merciful to others, while earthly wisdom puffs up the soul with pride and vanity.

This is wise and spiritual doctrine, grounded upon the truth, and leading unto the knowledge and service of God, and to familiarity with Him.

If you want to possess Him, you must get rid of earthly affections, not alone for persons, but for every creature, that you devote your mind to the Lord your God with your whole heart and with all your strength, freely, simply, without fear, trusting everything in entire confidence to His all-watchful Providence.[3]

Notes

[1] Prov. 8. 31.

[2] The exterior powers of a man are the imagination and passions; the interior his intelligence and will, which sometimes find themselves deprived of all the aids of sensible devotion.

[3] In truth, all the designs of God in our regard are full of mercy, and tend especially to our sanctification; the obstacles to these designs come only from our evil passions.

CHAPTER 7

On the Practice of Interior Recollection

The author of the book entitled *De Spiritu et Anima* tells us (chap. 21.)[1] that to ascend to God means nothing else than to enter into oneself. And, indeed, he who enters into the secret place of his own soul passes beyond himself, and does in very truth ascend to God.

Banish, therefore, from your heart the distractions of earth and turn your eyes to spiritual joys, that you may learn at last to repose in the light of the contemplation of God.

Indeed the soul's true life and her repose are to abide in God, held fast by love, and sweetly refreshed by the Divine consolations.

But many are the obstacles which hinder us from tasting this rest, and of our own strength we could never attain to it. The reason is evident—the mind is distracted and pre-occupied; it cannot enter into itself by the aid of the memory, for it is blinded by phantoms; nor can it enter by the intellect, for it is vitiated by the passions. Even the desire of interior joys and spiritual delights fails to draw it inward. It lies so deeply buried in things sensible and transitory that it cannot return to itself as to the image of God.

How needful is it, then, that the soul, lifted upon the wings of reverence and humble confidence, should rise

Symbol of faith.

Symbol of crucifixion

above itself and every creature by entire detachment, and should be able to say within itself: He Whom I seek, love, desire, among all, more than all, and above all, cannot be perceived by the senses or the imagination, for He is above both the senses and the understanding. He cannot be perceived by the senses, yet He is the object of all our desires; He is without shape, but He is supremely worthy of our heart's deepest love. He is beyond compare, and to the pure in heart greatly to be desired. Above all else is He sweet and love-worthy; His goodness and perfection are infinite.

When you understand this, your soul will enter into the darkness of the spirit, and will advance further and penetrate more deeply into itself.[2] You will by this means be able more speedily to see in a dark manner the Trinity in Unity, and Unity in Trinity, in Christ Jesus, in proportion as your effort is more inward; and the greater is your charity, the more precious the fruit will you reap. For the highest, in spiritual things, is ever that which is most interior. Grow not weary, therefore, and rest not from your efforts until you have received some foretaste of the fulness of joy that awaits you, and has obtained some first-fruits of the

Divine sweetness and delights.

Cease not in your pursuit until 'the God of gods will be seen in Sion.'[3]

In your spiritual ascent and in your search after a closer union with God you must not allow yourself to relax or slip back. But go forward until you have obtained the object of your desires. Follow the example of mountain-climbers. If your desires turn aside after the objects which pass below you will lose yourself in byways and countless distractions. Your mind will become dissipated and drawn in all directions by its desires. Your progress will be uncertain, you will not reach your goal, nor find rest after your labours.

If, on the other hand, the heart and mind, led on by love and desire, withdraw from the distractions of this world, and little by little abandon baser things to become recollected in the one true and unchangeable Good, to dwell there, held fast by the bonds of love, then you will grow strong, and your recollection will deepen the higher you rise on the wings of knowledge and desire.

They who have attained to this dwell as by habit in the Sovereign Good, and become at last inseparable from it.

True life, which is God Himself, becomes their inalienable possession;[4] for ever, free from all fear of the vicissitudes of time and change,[5] they rest in the peaceful enjoyment of this inward happiness, and in sweet communication with God. Their home is for ever fixed within their own souls, in Christ Jesus, Who is to all who come to Him 'the Way, and the Truth, and the Life'.[6]

NOTES

1 The book *De Spiritu et Anima* is of uncertain authorship. It is printed after the works of St. Augustine in Migne's *Patrologia Latina*, vol. 40., 779.

2 This darkness is the silence of the imagination, which no longer gains a hearing, and that of the intellect, which is sufficiently enlightened to understand that we can in reality understand nothing of the Divinity in itself, and that the best thing we can do is to remove from our conception of God all those limitations which we observe in creatures. The reason of this is that we can only know God naturally by means of what we see in creatures, and these are always utterly insufficient to give us an adequate idea of the Creator.

3 Ps. 84. 7.

4 We only lose God, the uncreated Good, by an unlawful attachment to created good; if we are free from this attachment, we tend to Him without effort.

5 The subsequent condemnation, in 1687, of this doctrine, as taught by Molino, could not, of course, be foreseen by Blessed Albertus writing in the thirteenth century.

6 John 14. 6.

The Lamb of God.

CHAPTER 8

That a Truly Devout Man should commit Himself to God in All Things

From all that has been said so far you have understood, if I am not mistaken, that the more you separate yourself from earthly images and created
objects, and the closer your union with God, the nearer
will you approach to the state of innocence and perfection. What could be happier, better, sweeter than this?

It is, therefore, of supreme importance that you should
preserve your soul so free from every trace or entanglement of earth that neither the world nor your friends, neither prosperity nor adversity, things present, past, or
future, which concern you or others, not even your own
sins above measure, should have power to trouble you.

Think only how you may live, as it were, alone with
God, removed from the world, the simple and pure life of
the spirit, as though your soul were already in eternity and
separated from your body.

There you would not busy yourself with earthly things,
nor be disquieted by the state of the world, by peace or
war, fair skies or foul, or anything here below. But you
would be absorbed and filled by His love.

Strive even now in this present life to detach from your
body and from every creature.

As far as you can, fix the eye of your soul steadfastly,
with unobscured gaze, upon the uncreated light.

Symbol of Hope.

Symbol of Peace.

Then will your soul, purified from the clouds of earth, be like an angel in a human body, no longer troubled by the flesh, or disturbed by vain thoughts.

Avoid temptations, persecutions, injuries, so that in adversity as in prosperity, you may still cling to God in unbroken peace.

When trouble, discouragement, confusion of mind trouble you, do not lose patience or be downhearted. Do not resort to vocal prayers or other consolations, but endeavour by an act of the will and reason to lift up your soul and unite it to God, whether your sensual nature will or no.

The devout soul should be so united to God, should so form and preserve her will in conformity to the Divine will, that she is no more occupied or allured by any creature than before it was created, but lives as though there existed but God and herself.[1]

She will receive in unvarying peace all that comes to her from the hand of Divine Providence. In all things she will hope in the Lord, without losing patience, peace, or silence.

Be aware, therefore, of how great value it is in the spiri-

Christ Pantocrator. Eleventh-century Byzantine fresco.

tual life to be detached from all things, that you may be interiorly united to God and conformed to Him.

Furthermore, there will then be no longer anything to intervene between your soul and God. From where could it come? Not from without, for the vow of voluntary poverty has despoiled you of all earthly goods, that of chastity has taken your body. Nor could it come from within, for obedience has taken from you your very will and soul. There is now nothing left which could come between God and yourself.

That you are a religious, your profession, your state, your habit and tonsure, and the other marks of the religious life declare. See to it whether you are a religious in truth or only one in name.

Consider how you are fallen and how you sinned against the Lord your God and against His justice if your deeds do not correspond with your holy state, if by will or desire you cling to the creature rather than to the Creator, or if you prefer the creature to the Creator.

NOTES

[1] And this she does because creatures no longer occupy her, except for God's sake.

CHAPTER 9

The Contemplation of God is to be preferred above All Other Exercises

Whatever exists outside of God is the work of His hands. Every creature is, therefore, a blending together of the actual and the possible, and as such is in its nature limited. Born of nothing, it is surrounded by nothingness, and tends to nothingness.[1]

Of necessity the creature depends each moment upon God, the supreme Artist, for its existence, preservation, power of action, and all that it possesses.

It is utterly unable to accomplish its own work, either for itself or for another, and is impotent as a thing which is not before that which is, the finite before the infinite. It follows, therefore, that our life, thoughts, and works should be in Him, of Him, for Him, and directed to Him, Who by the least sign of His will could produce creatures unspeakably more perfect than any which now exist.

It is impossible that there should be in the mind or heart a thought or a love more profitable, more perfect or more revered than those which rest upon God, the Almighty Creator, of Whom, in Whom, by Whom, towards Whom all tend.

From all eternity He contains within Himself the perfections of all things. There is nothing within Him which is not Himself. In Him and by Him exist the causes of all transitory things; in Him are the immutable origins of all things that change, whether rational or irrational.

All that happens in time has in Him its eternal principle.

He fills all; He is in all things by His essence, by which He is more present and more near to them than they are to themselves.[2]

In Him was life, and the life was the light of men.[3] It is true that the weakness of our understanding or our want of experience[4] may prompt us to make use of creatures in our contemplation, yet there is a kind of contemplation which is very fruitful, good, and real, which seems possible

Mosaic of Christ giving keys to St. Peter. Fifth-sixth century.

to all. Whether he meditates on the creature or the Creator, every man may reach the point at which he finds all his joy in His Creator, God, One in Trinity, and kindles the fire of Divine love in himself or in others, so as to merit eternal life.

We should notice here the difference which exists between the contemplation of Christians and that of pagan philosophers. The latter sought only their own perfection, and hence their contemplation affected their intellect only; they desired only to enrich their minds with knowledge. But the contemplation of Saints, which is that of Christians, seeks as its end the love of the God Whom they contemplate. Hence it is not content to find fruit for the intelligence, but penetrates beyond to the will that it may there enkindle love.

The Saints desired above all in their contemplation the increase of love.

It is better to know Jesus Christ and possess Him spiritually by grace, than, without grace, to have Him in the body, or even in His essence.

The more pure a soul becomes and the deeper her meditation, the clearer will be her inward vision. She now prepares, as it were, a ladder upon which she may ascend to the contemplation of God. This contemplation will set her on fire with love for all that is heavenly, Divine, eternal, and will cause her to despise as utter nothing all that is of time.

When we seek to arrive at the knowledge of God by the method of negation, we first remove from our conception of Him all that pertains to the body, the senses, the imagination. Then we reject even that which belongs to the reason, and the idea of being as it is found in creatures.[5] This, according to St. Denis, is the best means of attaining to the knowledge of God,[6] as far as it is possible in this world.

This is the darkness in which God dwells and into which Moses entered that he might reach the light inaccessible.[7]

But we must begin, not with the mind, but with the body. We must observe the accustomed order, and pass from the labour of action to the repose of contemplation, from the moral virtues to those of sublime contemplation.[8]

Why do you vainly wear yourself out in such multiplicity of things? It is of no value.

Seek and love only that perfect good which includes in itself all good, and that will be enough. You will be unhappy if you know and possess all, and are ignorant of this. If you knew at the same time both this good and all other things, this alone would make you happier. Therefore St. John has written: 'This is eternal life: that they may know thee,'[9] and the Prophet: 'I shall be satisfied with beholding your form.'[10]

NOTES

[1] This is so because, according to true philosophy, the essence of a thing is distinct from its existence.

[2] Every actual cause is more intimately present to its accomplished work than the work itself, which it necessarily precedes.

[3] John 1. 4.

[4] We cannot always experience Divine things, and at first we can only compare them to the things which we experience here below.

[5] We deny that there is in God anything which is a mere potentiality, or an imperfection. We deny in Him also the process of reasoning which is the special work of the faculty of reason, because this implies the absence of the vision of truth. We deny 'being as it is found in creatures,' because in creatures it is not necessarily limited, and subject to accident.

[6] 'Nom. Div.,' 1.

[7] Exod. 33. 2; Num. 12. 8; He. 3. 2.

[8] It would be well to quote St. Thomas, the disciple of Albert the Great, upon this important doctrine: 'A thing may be said to belong to the contemplative life in two senses, either as an essential part of it, or as a preliminary disposition. The moral virtues do not belong to the essence of contemplation, whose sole end is the contemplation of truth. .... But they belong to it as a necessary predisposition ... because they calm the passions and the tumult of exterior preoccupations, and so facilitate contemplation' ('Sum.,' 2, 2ac, q. 180, a. 2).

This distinction should never be lost sight of in reading the mystic books of the scholastics.

[9] John 17. 3.

[10] Ps. 17. 15.

CHAPTER 10

That we should Desire the Union of our Will with God

Seek not too eagerly after the grace of devotion, sensible sweetness and tears, but let your chief care be to remain inwardly united to God by good will in the intellectual part of the soul.[1]

Of a truth nothing is so pleasing to God as a soul freed from all trace and image of created things. A true religious should be at liberty from every creature that he may be wholly free to devote himself to God alone and cling to Him. Deny yourself, therefore, that you may follow Christ, your Lord and God, Who was truly poor, obedient, chaste, humble, and suffering, and Whose life and death were a scandal to many, as the Gospel clearly shows.[2]

The soul, when separated from the body, troubles not as to what becomes of the shell it has abandoned—it may be burnt, hanged, spoken evil of; and the soul is not afflicted by these outrages,[2] but thinks only of eternity and of the one thing necessary, of which the Lord speaks in the Gospel.[4]

So you should regard your body, as though the soul were already freed from it. Set ever before your eyes the eternal life in God, which awaits you, and think on that only good of which the Lord said: 'One thing is necessary.'[5]

A great grace will then descend upon your soul, which will help you in acquiring purity of mind and simplicity of heart.

And, indeed, this treasure is close at your doors. Turn from the images and distractions of earth, and you will learn what it is to be united to God without hindrance or impediment.

Then you will gain an unshaken constancy, which will strengthen you to endure all that may befall you.

So was it with the martyrs, the Fathers, the elect, and all the blessed. They despised all and thought only of possessing in God eternal security for their souls.

Armed within and united to God by a good will, they despised all that is of this world, as though their soul had already departed from the body.

Learn from them how great is the power of a good will united to God.

By that union of the soul with God it becomes, as it were, cut off from the flesh by a spiritual separation, and regards the outward man from afar as something alien to it.

Then, whatever may happen inwardly or in the body will be as little regarded as though it had befallen another person or a creature without reason.

He who is united to God is but one mind with Him.

Out of regard, therefore, for His sovereign honour, never be so bold as to think or imagine in His presence what you would blush to hear or see before men.

You ought to raise all your thoughts to God alone, and set Him before your inward gaze, as though He alone existed. You will then experience the sweetness of Divine union and even now make a true beginning of the life to come.

NOTES

[1] This admirable doctrine condemns a whole mass of insipid, shallow, affected and sensual books and ideas, which have in modern times flooded the world of piety, have banished from souls more wholesome thoughts, and filled them with a questionable and injurious sentimentality.

[2] Matt. 11. 6; 13. 57, etc.

[3] This shows an excellent grasp of the meaning of the celebrated maxim 'Perinde ac cadaver.'

[4] Luke 10. 42.

[5] Ibid.

CHAPTER 11

In What Manner we should resist Temptation and Endure Trials

He who with his whole heart draws towards God must of necessity be proved by temptation and trial.

When you feel temptation, by no means give your consent, but bear all with patience, sweetness, humility, and courage.

If you are tempted to blasphemy or any shameful sin, be well assured you can do nothing better than utterly to despise and condemn such thoughts. Blasphemy is indeed sinful, scandalous, and abominable, but do not be anxious about such temptations, but rather despise them, and do not let your conscience be troubled by them. The enemy will most certainly be put to flight if you condemn both him and his suggestions. He is too proud to endure scorn or contempt. The best remedy is, therefore, to trouble no more about these thoughts than we do about the flies which, against our will, dance before our eyes. Let not the servant of Christ therefore easily and needlessly lose sight of his Master's presence, nor let him grow impatient, murmur, or complain of these flies; I mean these light temptations, suspicions, sadness, depression, pusillanimity—mere nothings which a good will can put to flight by an elevation of the soul to God.

By a good will man makes God his Master, and the holy angels his guardians and protectors.

Good will drives away temptation as the hand brushes away a fly.

'Peace,' therefore, 'among men with whom he is pleased.'[1]

In truth no better gift than this can be offered to God.

Good will in the soul is the source of all good, the mother of all virtues. He who possesses it, possesses without fear of loss all he needs to live a good life.[2]

If you desire what is good and are not able to accomplish it,

God will reward you for it as though you had performed it.[3]

He has established as an eternal and unchangeable law that merit should lie in the will, and that upon the will should depend our future of Heaven or hell, reward or punishment.[4]

Love itself consists in nothing else but a strong will to serve God, a desire to please Him, and a fervent longing to enjoy Him.

Do not forget, therefore, temptation is not sin, but rather the means of proving virtue. By it man may gain great profit.[5] and this the more inasmuch as 'has not man a hard service upon earth.'[6]

NOTES

[1] Luke 2. 14.

[2] Nothing could be more conformable to the teaching of the Gospel than this doctrine.

At His birth Jesus bids the angels sing that peace belongs to men of good will (Luke 2. 14); later He will declare that His meat is to do the will of His Father (John 4. 34); that He seeks not His own will, but the will of Him Who sent Him (John 5. 30); that He came down from heaven to accomplish it (John 6. 38); and when face to face with death He will still pray that the Father's will be done, not His (Matt. 26. 39; Luke 22. 42). Over and over again, in the Gospel, do we find Him using the same language.

God answering Job out of the Whirlwind.
Engraving by William Blake(1757-1827)

He would have His disciples act in the same manner. It is not the man, He tells us, who repeats the words: 'My Father, my Father,' who shall enter into the Kingdom of Heaven, but he who does the will of God (Matt. 7. 21; Rom. 2. 13; Jas. 1. 22); and in the prayer which He dictates to us He bids us ask for the accomplishment of this will as the means of glorifying God, and of sanctifying our souls (Matt. 6. 10).

Finally, He tells us that if we conform ourselves to this sovereign will, we shall be His brethren (Matt. 12. 50; Mark 3. 35).

When certain persons, pious or otherwise, confusing sentiment with true love, ask themselves if they love God, or if they will be able to love Him always, we have only to ask them the same question in other words: Are they doing the will of God? can they do it—*i.e.*, can they perform their duty for God's sake? Put thus, the question resolves itself.

The reason for such a doctrine is very simple: to love anyone is to wish him well; that, in the case of God, is to desire His beneficent will towards us. Our Lord and Master recalled this principle when He said to His disciples, 'You are My friends, if you do the things that I command you' (John 15. 14).

3 We must, in virtue of the same principle, keep a firm hold of the truth, as indisputable as it is frequently forgotten, that we have the merit of the good which we will to carry out and are unable to accomplish, as we have also the demerit of the evil we should have done and could not.

4 'Upon the will depends our future of Heaven or hell,' because, given the knowledge of God, the will attaches itself to Him by love, or hates Him with obstinacy.

5 We may notice, in particular, a three-fold benefit: first, temptation calls for conflict, and so strengthens virtue; then it obliges a man to adhere deliberately to that virtue which is assailed by the temptation, and so gain a further perfection; finally, there are necessarily included in both the conflict and the adherence to good numerous virtuous, and therefore meritorious, acts. Thus we may reap advantage from temptation both in our dispositions and our acts.

6 Job 7. 1.

CHAPTER 12

The Power of the Love of God

All that we have so far described, all that is necessary for salvation, can find in love alone its highest, completest, most beneficent perfection.

Love supplies all that is wanting for our salvation; it contains abundantly every good thing, and lacks not even the presence of the supreme object of our desires.

It is by love alone that we turn to God, are transformed into His likeness, and are united to Him, so that we become one spirit with Him, and receive by and from Him all our happiness: here in grace, hereafter in glory. Love can find no rest till she rests in the full and perfect possession of the Beloved.

It is by the path of love, that God gets closer to man, and man to God, but where love is not found God cannot dwell. If, then, we possess love we possess God, for 'God is love.'[1]

There is nothing keener than love, nothing more subtle, nothing more penetrating. Love cannot rest till it has

Opening the fold. Engraving by Samuel Palmer.

sounded all the depths and learnt the perfections of its Beloved. It desires to be one with Him, and, if it could, would form but one being with the Beloved. It is for this reason that it cannot suffer anything to intervene between it and the object loved, which is God, but springs forward towards Him, and finds no peace till it has overcome every obstacle, and reached even unto the Beloved.

Love has the power of uniting and transforming; it transforms the one who loves into him who is loved, and him who is loved into him who loves. Each passes into the other, as far as it is possible.

And first consider the intelligence. How completely love transports the loved one into him who loves! With what sweetness and delight the one lives in the memory of the other, and how earnestly the lover tries to know, not superficially but intimately, all that concerns the object of his love, and strives to enter as far as possible into his inner life!

Think next of the will, by which also the loved one lives in him who loves. Does he not dwell in him by that tender affection, that sweet and deeply-rooted joy which he feels? On the other hand, the lover lives in the beloved by the sympathy of his desires, by sharing his likes and dislikes, his joys and sorrows, until the two seem to form but one. Since 'love is strong as death,'[2] it carries the lover out of himself into the heart of the beloved, and holds him prisoner there.

The soul is more truly where it loves than where it gives life, since it exists in the object loved by its own nature, by reason and will; whilst it is in the body it animates only by bestowing on it an existence which it shares with the animal creation.[3]

There is, therefore, but one thing which has power to draw us from outward objects into the depths of our own

(Above) The Rising Moon; and (below) The Lovely Tower.
Both engravings by Samuel Palmer.

souls, there to form an intimate friendship with Jesus. Nothing but the love of Christ and the desire of His sweetness can lead us thus to feel, to comprehend and experience the presence of His Divinity.

The power of love alone is able to lift up the soul from earth to the heights of Heaven, nor is it possible to ascend to eternal beatitude except on the wings of love and desire.

Love is the life of the soul, its nuptial garment, its perfection.[4]

Upon love are based the law, the prophets, and the precepts of the Lord.[5] Hence the Apostle wrote to the Romans: ' Therefore love is the fulfilling of the law,'[6] and in the first Epistle to Timothy: 'The aim of our charge is love.'[7]

NOTES

[1] 1 John 4. 8.

[2] Cant.(from the Douay translation) 8. 6.

[3] The author is speaking here of the soul in so far as it is human, and it is as such that it is more where it loves than where it gives life.

[4] Without charity there is no perfect virtue, since without it no virtue can lead man to his final end, which is God, although it may lead him to some lower end. It is in this sense that, according to the older theologians, charity is the 'form' of the other virtues, since by it the acts of all the other virtues are supernaturalized and directed to their true end—*i.e.*, to God. *Cf.* St. Th. 'Sum.,' 2, 2[ae], q. 23, aa. 7, 8.

[5] Matt. 22. 40.

[6] Rom. 13. 10.

[7] I Tim. 1. 5.

CHAPTER 13

Of the Nature and Advantages of Prayer — Of Interior Recollection

We are utterly unable to attain to love or any other good thing by ourselves. We have nothing to offer to the Lord, the Author of all, which was not His already.

One thing alone remains to us: that in every occurrence we should turn to Him in prayer, as He Himself taught us by word and example. Let us go to Him as guilty, poor, and miserable, as beggars, weak and needy, as subjects and slaves, yet as His children.

By ourselves we are utterly destitute. What can we do but throw ourselves at His feet in deepest humility, holy fear mingling in our souls with love, peace, and recollection?

And while we are glad to draw close with all lowliness and modesty, with minds sincere and simple, let our hearts burn with great desires, with ardour and heartfelt longings. And so let us pray to our God, and lay before Him with entire confidence the perils which menace us on every side. Let us freely, unhesitatingly, and in all simplicity, confide ourselves to Him, and offer Him our whole being, even to the last fibre, for are we not in truth absolutely His?

Let us keep nothing for ourselves, and then will be fulfilled in us the saying of Blessed Isaac, one of the Fathers of the Desert who, speaking of this kind of prayer, said: 'We shall be one being with God, and He will be all in all to us, when that perfect charity by which He loved us first has entered into our inmost hearts.'[1]

This will be accomplished when God alone becomes the object of all our love, our desires, our striving, of all our efforts and thoughts, of all that we behold, speak of, hope for; when that union which exists between the Father and the Son, and between the Son and the Father shall be found also in our mind and soul.

Angel holding a book. From an engraving by Eric Gill (1882-1940).

Since His love for us is so pure, sincere, and unchanging, ought not we in return to give Him a love constant and uninterrupted?

So intimate should be our union with Him that our hopes, thoughts, prayers breath only God.[2] The truly spiritual man should set before him, as the goal of all his efforts and desires, the possession even in a mortal body, of an image of the happiness to come, and the enjoyment even here below of some foretaste of the delights, the life, and glory of Heaven.

This, I say, is the end of all perfection—that the soul may become so purified from every earthly longing, and so raised to spiritual things, that at last the whole life and the desires of the heart form one unbroken prayer.

When the soul has shaken off the dust of earth and

The Tree of Jesse. Late twelfth century.

aspires unto her God, to Whom the true religious ever
directs his intention, dreading the least separation from
Him as a most cruel death; when peace reigns within and
she is delivered from the bondage of her passions and
cleaves with firmest purpose to the one Sovereign Good,

then will be fulfilled in her the words of the Apostle: 'Pray constantly,'[3] and 'in every place, lifting holy hands, without anger and quarrelling.'[4]

When once this purity of soul has gained the victory over man's natural inclination for the things of sense, when all earthly longings are quenched and the soul is, as it were, transformed into the likeness of pure spirits or angels, then all she receives, all she undertakes, all she does, will be a pure and true prayer.

Only persevere faithfully in your efforts and, as I have shown from the beginning, it will become as simple and easy for you to contemplate God and rejoice in Him in your recollection as to live a purely natural life.

NOTES

[1] Good can only love Himself or creatures for His own sake; if we have this love within our souls we shall be in a certain sense one being with Him.

[2] This teaching is based on the definition that prayer is essentially 'an elevation of the soul to God.'

[3] 1 Thess. 5. 17.

[4] 1 Tim. 2. 8.

CHAPTER 14

That Everything should be Judged according to our Conscience

There is also another practice which will tend greatly to your progress in spiritual perfection, and will aid you to gain purity of soul and tranquil rest in God. Whatever men say or think of you, bring it to your own conscience. Enter within yourself, and there, turning a deaf ear to all else, set yourself to learn the truth. Then you will see clearly that the praise and honour of men bring no profit, but rather loss, if you know that you are guilty and worthy of condemnation in the sight of truth. And, just as it us useless to be honoured outwardly by men if your conscience accuse you within, so in like manner is it no loss to you if men despise, blame, or persecute without, if within you are innocent and free from reproach or blame. Rather, you then have great reason to rejoice in the Lord in patience, silence and peace.

Adversity is powerless to harm where sin has no dominion; and just as there is no evil which goes unpunished, so is there no good without recompense.

Seek not with the hypocrites your reward and crown from men, but rather from the hand of God, not now, but hereafter; not for a passing moment, but for eternity.

You can, therefore, do nothing higher nor better in every tribulation or occurrence than enter into the sanctuary of your soul, and there call upon the Lord Jesus Christ, your helper in temptation and affliction. There you should humble yourself, confessing your sins, and praising your God and Father, Who both chastises and consoles.

There decide to accept with unruffled peace, readiness, and confidence from the hands of God's unfailing Providence and marvellous wisdom all that is sent you of prosperity or adversity whether touching yourself or others. Then you will obtain remission of your sins;[1] bitterness will be driven from your soul, sweetness and confidence will penetrate it, grace and mercy will descend upon it. Then a sweet familiarity will draw you on and strengthen you, abundant consolation will flow to you from the bosom of God. You will then adhere to Him and form an indissoluble union with Him.

But beware of imitating hypocrites who, like the Pharisees, try to appear outwardly before men more holy than they know themselves in truth to be. Is it not utter folly to seek or desire human praise and glory for oneself or others, while within we are filled with shameful and grievous sins? Assuredly he who pursues such vanities can hope for no share in the good things of which we spoke just now, but shame will infallibly be his lot.

Keep your worthlessness and your sins ever before your eyes, and learn to know yourself that you may grow in humility.

Do not shrink from being regarded by all the world as filthy mud, vile and abject, on account of your grievous sins and defects. Consider yourself among others as dross in the midst of gold, as tares in the wheat, straw among the grain, as a wolf among the sheep, as Satan among the children of God.

Neither should you desire to be respected by others, or preferred to anyone whatsoever. Fly rather with all your strength of heart and soul from that pestilential poison, the venom of praise, from a reputation founded on boasting and ostentation, lest, as the prophet says, 'The sinner is praised in the desires of his soul.[2]

Again, in Isaiah, we read: 'Your leaders mislead you, and confuse the course of your paths.'[3] Also the Lord says: 'Woe to you when all men speak well of you!'[4]

NOTES

[1] Remission may be obtained in this way of the fault in the case of venial sins, of the punishment due in all sins. [2] Ps. 9. 24. [3] Isa. 3. 12. [4] Luke 6. 26.

CHAPTER 15

On the Contempt of Self: How it is Acquired: Its Profit to the Soul

The more truly a man knows his own misery, the more fully and clearly does he behold the majesty of God. The more vile he is in his own eyes for the sake of God, of truth, and of justice, the more worthy of esteem is he in the eyes of God.

Strive earnestly, therefore, to look on yourself as utterly contemptible, to think yourself unworthy of any benefit, to be displeasing in your own eyes, but pleasing to god. Desire that others should regard you as vile and mean.

Learn not to be troubled in tribulations, afflictions, injuries; not to be incensed against those that inflict them, nor to entertain thoughts of resentment against them. Try, on the contrary, sincerely to believe yourself worthy of all injuries, contempt, ill-treatment and scorn.

In truth, he who for God's sake is filled with sorrow and guilt dreads to be honoured and loved by another. He does not refuse to be an object of hatred, or shrink from being trodden under foot and despised as long as he lives, in order that he may practise real humility and cleave in purity of heart to God alone.

It does not require exterior labour or bodily health to love God only, to hate oneself more than all, to desire to seem little in the eyes of others: what is needed is rather repose of the senses, the effort of the heart, silence of the mind.

It is by labouring with the heart, by the inward aspiration of the soul, that you will learn to forsake the base things of earth and to rise to what is heavenly and Divine.

You will then become transformed in God, and this the more speedily if, in all sincerity, without condemning or despising your neighbour, you desire to be regarded by all as a reproach and scandal—even to be abhorred as filthy mire, rather than possess the delights of earth, or be honoured and exalted by men, or enjoy any advantage or happiness in this fleeting world.

Have no other desire in this perishable life of the body, no other consolation than unceasingly to weep over, regret and detest your offences and faults.

Learn utterly to despise yourself to annihilate yourself and to appear daily more contemptible in the eyes of others.

Strive to become even more unworthy in your own eyes, in order to please God alone, to love Him only and cling to Him.

Concern not yourself with anything except thy Lord Jesus Christ, Who ought to reign alone in your affections. Have no solicitude or care except for Him Whose power and Providence give moment and being to all things.[1]

It is not now the time to rejoice but rather to lament with all the sincerity of your heart.

If you cannot weep, sorrow at least that you have no tears to shed; if you can, grieve the more because by the gravity of your offences and number of your sins you are yourself the cause of your grief. A man under sentence of death does not trouble himself as to the dispositions of his executioners; so he who truly mourns and sheds the tears of repentance, refrains from delight, anger, vain-glory, indignation, and every like passion.

The life and conduct of those whose faults call for sighs and tears should not resemble those of men who have remained innocent and have nothing to expiate.

Were it otherwise, how would the guilty, great though their crimes may have been, differ in their punishment and expiation from the innocent? Iniquity would then be more free than innocence. Renounce all, therefore, condemn all, separate yourself from all, that you may lay deep the foundations of sincere penance.

He who truly loves Jesus Christ, and sorrows for Him, who bears Him in his heart and in his body, will have no thought, or care, or consideration for anything else. Such a one will sincerely mourn over his sins and offences, will long after eternal happiness, will remember the Judgment and will think diligently on his last end in lowly fear. He, then, who wishes to arrive speedily at a state of contentment and to reach God, counts that day lost on which he has not been ill-spoken of and despised.

What is this contentment but freedom from the vices and passions, purity of heart, the attainment of virtue?

Count yourself as already dead, since you must die some day.

And now, but one word more. Let this be the test of your thoughts, words, and deeds. If they render you more humble, more recollected in God, more strong, then they are according to God. But if you find it otherwise, then fear in case all is not according to God, acceptable to Him, or profitable to yourself.

NOTES

[1] St. Thomas explains as follows both the possibility and the correctness of this opinion of ourselves: 'A man can, without falsehood, believe and declare himself viler than all others, both on account of the secret faults which he knows to exist within him, and on account of the gifts of God hidden in the souls of others.'

St. Augustine, in his work *De Virginit.*, ch. 52., says: 'Believe that others are better than you in the depths of their souls, although outwardly you may appear better than they.'

In the same way one may truthfully both say and believe that one is altogether useless and unworthy in his own strength. The Apostle says (2 Cor. 3. 5): 'Not that we are sufficient to think anything of ourselves, as of ourselves, but our sufficiency is from God' ('Sum.,' 2, 2ae, q. 161, a. 6, 1m).

The Plains of Heaven. Engraving by John Martin (1789-1854).

CHAPTER 16

Of the Providence of God, which watches over All Things

Do you want to draw closer to God without obstruction or hindrance, freely and in peace, as we have described? Do you want to be united and drawn to Him in a union so close that it will endure in prosperity and adversity, in life and in death? Do not delay to commit all things with trustful confidence into the hands of His sure and infallible Providence.

Is it not most fitting that you should trust Him Who gives to all creatures, in the first place, their existence, power, and movement, and, secondly, their species and nature, ordering in all their number, weight, and measure?

Just as Art presupposes the operations of Nature, so Nature presupposes the work of God, the Creator, Preserver, Organiser, and Administrator.

To Him alone belong infinite power, wisdom, and goodness, essential mercy, justice, truth, and charity, immutable eternity, and immensity. Nothing can exist and act of its own power, but every creature acts of necessity by the power of God, the first moving cause, the first principle

Visionary drawing by John Flaxman to illustrate Canto Thirteen of *Paradise* from Dante's *The Divine Comedy*

and origin of every action, Who acts in every active being.

If we consider the ordered harmony of the universe, it is the Providence of God which must arrange all things, even to the smallest details.

From the infinitely great to the infinitely small nothing can escape His eternal Providence; nothing has been drawn from His control, either in the acts of free-will, in events we ascribe to chance or fate, or in what has been designed by Him. We may go further: it is as impossible for God to make anything which does not fall within the dominion of His Providence as it is for Him to create anything which is not subject to His action. Divine Providence, therefore, extends over all things, even the thoughts of man.

This is the teaching of Holy Scripture, for in the Epistle of St. Peter it is written: 'Cast all your anxieties on Him, for He has cares about you.'[1]

And, again, the Prophet says: 'Cast your burden on the Lord and He will sustain you.'[2] Also in Ecclesiasticus we read: 'My children, behold the generations of men; and know that no one has hoped in the Lord, and has been confounded. For who has continued in His commandment, and has been forsaken?'[3] And the Lord says: 'Therefore do not be anxious, saying, what shall we eat?'[4] All that you can hope for from God, however great it may be, you shall without doubt receive, according to the promise in Deuteronomy: 'Every place on which the sole of your foot treads shall be yours.'[5] As much as you can desire you shall receive, and as far as the foot of your confidence reaches, so far you shall possess.

Hence St. Bernard says: 'God, the Creator of all things, is so full of mercy and compassion that whatever may be the grace for which we stretch out our hands, we shall not fail to receive it.'[6]

It is written in St. Mark: 'Whatsoever you shall ask when you pray, believe that you shall receive, and they shall come unto you.'[7]

The greater and more persistent your confidence in God, and the more earnestly you turn to Him in lowly reverence, the more you shall abundantly and certainly receive all you can ask.

But if, on account of the number and importance of his sins, the confidence of any should languish, let him who feels this torpor remember that all is possible to God, that what He wills must infallibly happen, and what He does not will cannot come to pass, and, finally, that it is as easy for Him to forgive and blot out innumerable and heinous sins as to forgive one.

On the other hand, it is just as impossible for a sinner to deliver himself from a single sin as it would be for him to raise and cleanse himself from many sins; for, not only are we unable to accomplish this, but by ourselves we cannot even think what is right.[8] All comes to us from God. It is, however, far more dangerous, other things being equal, to be entangled in many sins than to be held only by one.

In truth, no evil remains unpunished, and for every mortal sin is due, in strict justice, an infinite punishment, because a mortal sin is committed against God, to Whom belong infinite greatness, dignity, and glory.

Moreover, according to the Apostle, 'the Lord knows who are His,'[9] and it is impossible that one of them should perish, no matter how violently the tempests and waves of error rage, how great the scandal, schisms and persecutions, how grievous the adversities, discords, heresies, tribulations, or temptations of every kind.

The number of the elect and the measure of their worth is eternally and unalterably predestined. So true is this that all the good and evil which can happen to them or to others, all prosperity and adversity, serve only to their advantage.

Furthermore, adversity does but render them more glorious, and proves their fidelity more surely. Delay not, therefore, to commit all things without fear to the Providence of God, by Whose permission all evil of whatever kind happens, and ever for some good end. It could not be except He permitted it; its form and measure are allowed by Him Who can and will by His wisdom turn all to good.

Just as it is by His action that all good is wrought, so is it by His permission that all evil happens.[10]

But from the evil He draws good, and therefore marvellously shows His power, wisdom, and clemency by our Lord Jesus Christ. He also shows His mercy and His justice, the power of grace, the weakness of nature, and the beauty of the universe. So He shows by the force of contrast the glory of the good, and the malice and punishment of the wicked.

In like manner, in the conversion of a sinner we see contrition, confession, and penance; and, on the other hand, the tenderness of God, His mercy and love, His glory and His goodness.

Yet sin does not always turn to the good of those who commit it; but it is usually the greatest of perils and worst of ills, for it causes the loss of grace and glory. It stains the soul and provokes punishment even for eternity. From so great an evil may our Lord Jesus preserve us! Amen.

NOTES

[1] 1 Pet. 5. 7.

[2] Ps. 54. 23.

[3] Ecclus.(from the Douay translation) 2. 11, 12.

[4] Matt. 6. 31.

[5] Deut. 11. 24.

[6] *Cf.* Serm. 1. in Pent.

[7] Mark 11. 24.

[8] 2 Cor. 3. 5.

[9] 2 Tim. 2. 19.

[10] The teaching of Albert the Great on Divine Providence is truly admirable. It is based upon the axiom that the actions of the creature do not depend partly upon itself and partly upon God, but wholly upon itself and wholly upon God (*cf.* St. Thomas 'Cont. Gent.,' 3. 70).

Human causality is not parallel with the Divine, but subordinate to it, as the scholastics teach. This doctrine alone safeguards the action of God and of that of the creature. The doctrine of parallelism derogates from both, and leads to fatalism by attributing to God things which He has not done, and suppressing for man the necessary principle of all good, especially that of liberty.

It is the doctrine of subordinated causes also which explains how things decreed by God are determined by the supreme authority, and infallibly come to pass, without prejudice to the freedom of action of secondary causes. All this belongs to the highest theology. Unhappily, certain modern authors have forgotten it.

Title page by William Blake.